CONQUER
STAGE FRIGHT

A FIELD GUIDE TO
EXCELLENCE IN PERFORMANCE

Practical Help
For
Athletes, Speakers, Musicians
& All Who Perform for the Public

Richard H. Cox M.D., Ph.D., D.Min.

RESOURCE *Publications* • Eugene, Oregon

Resource Publications
A division of Wipf and Stock Publishers
199 W 8th Ave, Suite 3
Eugene, OR 97401

Conquer Stage Fright
Practical Help for Athletes, Speakers, Musicians,
and All Who Perform for the Public
By Cox, Richard H., MD, PhD
Copyright©2009 by Cox, Richard H., MD, PhD
ISBN 13: 978-1-60899-568-4
Publication date 4/16/2010

TABLE OF CONTENTS

DEDICATION

This book is dedicated to my life-time mentor, the Rev. Dr. Vernon Grounds, Chancellor of Denver Seminary, and his devoted wife, Ann, who helped me as a struggling teenager to overcome a lack of self-confidence, and performance anxiety that caused me to literally shake, and gave my trumpet playing entirely too much vibrato, when standing before a group. Now with both of them in their 95th year, and on the day of this writing, I asked him what he and Ann, his pianist/organist wife, saw in me that motivated them to give so much to me. Still mentally sharp and crisp in thinking as ever, he simply said, "potential." Words will never thank them enough for helping to push me over a wall that I could not climb by myself.

PREFACE

After giving hundreds of seminars, workshops, clinics, and private consultations, many things have become apparent to me regarding what is commonly called "stage fright." This phenomenon is shared by musicians, ministers, teachers, athletes, and all who find themselves in the "spotlight." Regardless of the level of one's training and performance, there are common elements for all performers. I have worked with beginning students who have been traumatized after their first "solo" performance on a musical instrument, and with professionals who have been in the field and are recognized as highly accomplished. Some of these persons have been in the field of music, others in public/motivational speaking, athletic competition, and highly educated professors and teachers who know their subject expertly well, but literally shake when required to present before a group of peers.

Performance anxiety/stage-fright, is without doubt the number one enemy of most performers, whether in music, athletic competition, or public speaking. It does not need to be so. Understanding and dealing with the psychological, physical, and spiritual aspects of behavior presented in this book will give practical, down-to-earth specific techniques and practices to overcome this disabling enemy.

No individual is like any other individual in the causation, the expression, or the remediation necessary to overcome this devastating disorder. I consider it a "disorder" rather than a habit or reaction, since it is grounded in the very personality, neurological functioning, and psychological make up of the person.

Like any disorder, proper diagnosis is essential. Diagnosis is not usually a personal task. It is difficult to "see what is wrong" with ourselves. I have worked with seasoned professionals who have "looked right at the problem – and sometimes the answer - without "seeing it." Once it is pointed out, they "see it" immediately. However, by the time they recognize it as a problem, it is so ingrained that, even though they know what to do and help others with the same problem, they are unable to change their own problem alone.

This is where some other seasoned professional is needed. You will find, in reading this text, that most all problems are not "simple," one-answer situations. They usually involve much more than meets the eye. If it were that simple, most persons would have solved the problem by now. This is where a multi-disciplinary professional is often needed, one who understands the physiology, the psychology, and your specific performance form. Attempting to change deeply ingrained behaviors incorrectly not only frequently fail, but, more seriously, seldom address what is needed to see the whole problem. It is essential, when seeking help, to get the appropriate referral. Attempts to solve the problem with incorrect approaches have ended the career of more than one performer. This short text is intended to offer a common sense approach to facing this disorder and finding the answer that fits you. There is no "one size fits all" answer. However, now in my eighth decade of life and having worked with literally thousands of such individuals in a period of over 50 years, I have yet to encounter an individual who intently works at doing so who cannot overcome stage fright and find their individual path to excellence in performance.

There have been many fine books written on the technical aspects of performance, including the neurological understanding of all sorts of behavior including anxiety and performance. This book is not intended to be one of that nature; but rather, to offer practical, very doable answers to some of the problems encountered by those suffering from this disorder. This text will not replace professional help when needed, but will provide a solid basis from which to start the journey of solving the problem. For additional and more detailed information, readers are encouraged to read the more in-depth writings that are listed in the references.

Richard H. Cox, MD, PhD, D.Min
Chapel Hill, North Carolina
2009

LESSON ONE
What is stage fright?

When a person says, "I have stage fright," they usually mean that, when called upon to perform before an audience, they are nervous and manifest any multitude of symptoms. Sometimes they literally physically shake, break out in a cold sweat, get dizzy, have a headache, get 'butterflies,' become nauseous, or have toilet urgencies. Some suffer from visual blurriness or get goose bumps, and many more very troubling physical and mental symptoms. Often times they suffer memory lapses and actually forget what they have perfectly well prepared to say or perform.

If you have some of theses symptoms and find yourself described as above, this book is for you. However, reading it will not change the condition. It will require careful attention to your individual problem, specific attention to the underlying foundation of that problem, and the willingness to work diligently to change many things including attitude, behavior, and sometimes even lifestyle, including more physical and mental aspects than you have probably ever considered were part of this condition.

Webster's dictionary defines "fright" as "fear, terror, and alarm." All of those words have been experienced by the person who has stage fright. It is clear that Mr. Webster never experienced this condition himself, since he defines "stage fright" as "nervousness felt when appearing as a speaker or performer before an audience." Those who are acquainted with this disorder would never define the condition as this mild.

The term "performance anxiety" might better describe what most persons who have this condition feel. Webster's dictionary defines "anxiety" in a bit more understood language: "uneasy, apprehensive, worried... abnormal state of feeling powerless... unable to cope, sweating, trembling..."

Whether you call your dis-ease "stage fright" or "performance anxiety," the feelings, symptoms and resulting inability to present your finest talent and skill will be the same.

To attach the word "stage" to the fright experience is a misnomer. No one actually fears the stage. They fear what might happen when they are on the stage. This distinction is vital since it is an abnormal reaction to what has not yet occurred, but which, in the imagination, might. The anxiety which is aroused is abnormal since it is based on anticipation, not on fact. Further, the element of "fright" is usually a frame being played from an old tape somewhere in the person's background. The experience, whether real or hyper-memorialized from something that has happened before, has "grown" and has doubtless become embellished since that time. That which underlies the present "fear" may have occurred even in early childhood. All memories change over time; some morph into memories enhanced to be happy which were not at all that great... but, unfortunately, most negative memories continue to grow negatively. Simple mistakes in childhood often cripple adults due to the incredible size and importance they have become.

However, each time the tape is played, the memory becomes more vivid and less accurate. The mind then works at its most prolific ability and creative best by "making up the story" that becomes real in your mind – and possibly becomes your downfall.

Stage fright, then, is not real... and yet *is* incredibly real! It is a replay with a million ornamentations that hinder excellence in performance. The brain is being literally warped by imprinting this experience on it's ledger of life as your "normal, and expected" method of handling things you cannot predict. Many times this will be one experience replayed a thousand times, hence interpreted as what happens "all the time." Anxiety is the art of making real the imaginary!

Many persons are actually capable of presenting or performing with minimal "stage fright," yet have so accepted anxiety as their norm as to expect it next time. And, of course, the "expected" happens. Psychologists speak of "self-fulfilling prophecy," meaning that which we expect, we plan for, and actually accomplish, in fulfilling what we have expected. It is amazing that the human brain should be capable of this kind of self-destruction and performance sabotage, but it is.

You will learn in later chapters of this book how the body accommodates the mind, and how the mind assists the body in carrying out actions, even those that are not healthy and productive – or even what we think are satisfying. Strangely, when the mind has succeeded in failing – it has succeeded. But it has succeeded in failing!

When you witness yourself or someone else being "nervous" on the stage, you may jump to the conclusion that they are suffering from "stage fright." It may not be. There are many causes for such reactions and many of them are incredibly subtle. Others are buried in other seemingly innocuous elements such as diet.

Whatever the cause, and whatever the price to correct it, it must be done. Excess anxiety is not healthy for anyone, a performer or not. The body responds to threat with psychological and physical symptoms that can be anywhere from irritating to life-threatening as a result of excess anxiety. Whether teaching, performing, working on a lathe in a machine shop, climbing a ladder to paint a house, or singing an aria at the "Met," performance anxiety will lessen your degree of excellence in whatever you are doing.

Although this book speaks primarily to the "performer", and tends to see "performance" as a public demonstration in the arts, the same principles apply to anyone in any walk of life. We are all called upon to "be our best" and to strive for excellence in all that we do.

LESSON TWO

Where is the problem?

We must look at what might be called "trigger points" of this disorder. Frequently a performer feels confident, relaxed, and completely without worry a few minutes before the appearance, then literally falls apart only seconds before the performance. There are many "trigger points" that you will learn about in subsequent chapters. For now, it is important to think about the phenomenon of "trigger points." Where you hurt is often a different place than the actual injury. Reactions occur all along the nervous and musculo-skeletal system when injured. As a result, you can get a headache when you hit your thumb with a hammer!

Also, an actual injury does not have to occur at all. Just the threat of one can cause the body to prepare for war. It sets up defenses in the form of histaminic responses like hives on the skin, heart responses like a quickening of the pulse rate, shortness of breath, vascular reactions such as blushing, and even what is called "hyperhydrosis" – excessive sweating. These reactions are normal. Anticipation causes an arousal of the autonomic nervous system, which is normal. Therefore, what is called "anxiety" in minimal amounts is normal. However, it should not be called anxiety. Anxiety, as such, is a normal but exaggerated response to anticipated threat. Performing should not be a threat. The body knows how to deal with anticipation and the arousal that comes from it. Further, the body prepares for it and "sets you up" to handle it. However, when the mind becomes overactive and "feeds" itself with all those past experiences - bad feeling tapes, and memories

– anticipation becomes anxiety and goes out of control.

Sometimes we can pin-point the cause of the anxiety - but mostly not. Most of the time it is better called "free-floating" anxiety, meaning that we just can't pin it down to any one thing or even any one set of things. This makes it very difficult to deal with, since we all want simple answers... and we want them now! When dealing with a generalized pattern, we tend to take the "shot-gun" approach, hoping that something will work. Mostly it does not. In actuality, the pellets from the shot gun produce other holes that cause further damage. This is seen particularly in students who have been told, "Just settle down, everything will be fine." The student knows that the wisdom producer is lying because they know they are not prepared, have not adequately practiced, don't have the underlying self-confidence, or a myriad of other things that they know to be true.

Encouraging a person to believe that they can excel in the face of willful negligence is both dishonest and sets up a neurotic pattern for unrealistic outcomes.

As has been mentioned, early experiences are incredibly important. I attended a grade-schooler's piano recital recently. A little guy, probably not more than 6 years old, confidently strode to the stage, asked the audience to stand for the national anthem, then sat down and played the Star Spangled Banner. He was playing from memory and in the middle of it, he forgot the notes. He simply looked around, not at all flustered, and found his way back to the right notes. There was no sign of anxiety or embarrassment in the least. He bowed and left the stage confidently. He was followed shortly thereafter by a young lady, probably around

9 or 10, who forgot her piece and also eventually found her way back to the score, but fell apart and wept throughout the remainder of the recital, unwilling to be comforted by her understanding mother and father sitting beside her.

In the first incidence, we must look at the underlying personality factors, parental expectations, and self-confidence of the young performer. By all likelihood this youngster will not develop "stage fright." He did not seem to "take negative pictures" of the event and his future tapes will not play that experience as "bad." The second performer has probably now already developed the basis for stage fright, and has imprinted this performance as a standard in her unconscious and even conscious mind. They will both play the tape of their performance over and over in their heads. The first one will smile and the second one will cry. The next time they approach the stage, one will feel confident and self-assured and the other will expect to fail, and may well do so.

There is such a thing as too much self-confidence. It is possible to be arrogant and display an unhealthy ego. We have all seen plenty of this in athletes, musicians and public speakers. Humility is a valuable asset in one's personality bank when in proper amounts. There is a famous story told of a young preacher who strode over-confidently and arrogantly up to the platform to preach, but forgot his lines, made a fool of himself, and, with much embarrassment, slowly descended the platform with his "tail between his legs." An older and wiser deacon comforted and admonished him by saying, "young man, had you gone up the way you came down, you might have come down the way you went up." How true.

It is helpful to sit quietly and reminisce about one's life. How did we develop our attitudes, behaviors, fears, and expectations? Did we have encouragement as we struggled to learn, or were we discouraged? Were we compared to a sibling, a neighbor, or to an imaginary ideal? Did we learn to play an instrument to please a parent? Did we learn to live out a parent's personal failed aspirations?

I am reminded of a young man with whom I worked. His father was a demanding, arrogant person who had personally failed at playing the trumpet well, although he continued to struggle with it into adulthood. His son was an introvert, obviously badgered and extremely fearful of his father. He did not want to play a trumpet. But play a trumpet he would, whether he wanted to or not, just to please his father. He was obviously being forced to live out his father's failed trumpet-playing aspirations. No instrument was too costly for his son. He bought one after another, "giving" it to his son. His son did not want a trumpet at all! His father took the son to one teacher after another, with all of them "giving up" and recognizing that this youngster did not have any interest in learning to play a trumpet. Finally, the young man was brought to me to see what the "problem" was. Of course, diagnosis in this case was easy – the answer, however, was not what the father wanted to hear. The son felt relieved, but knew that his father would not accept the answer – which he did not. At last sighting, the father was still seen leading his son to one teacher after another and one trumpet salesperson to another, attempting to cajole, force, or otherwise bribe his now teen-age son into fulfilling a father's personal dream!

Diagnosing the problem must seek balance. One should not become so complacent as to become over-assured. All performances, whether musical, speaking engagements, or athletic events, are fraught with the unexpected and the necessity to be ready to change plans. A musician may have rehearsed a piece perfectly in the key of F Major, only to find on the day of performance that the guest singer wishes it to be in A Major – or "Z Minor!"). There can be no excuses – transposing and changing the key signature is a must. The public speaker finds that there is a faulty microphone, terrible room arrangement, everything is going wrong that could possibly be. It doesn't matter – the speech must be given. The athlete likewise, finds that the playing field has changed overnight. The show must go on!

Adaptability, looking at alternatives, having some "secrets of performance" in one's pocket, being ready for the unexpected, and learning to enjoy the ability to alter your "usual and customary" way of doing things is essential. The secret is balance. How does one attain a healthy sense of self-respect, self-confidence, and expectation for success without becoming arrogant or overly proud? The following chapters will give you the basis upon which to make the decisions and put into practice the habits that will guarantee exceptional success without being haughty, superficial, or arrogant.

So then, what is stage fright? It is the neurotic expectations of the unknown based upon imaginary results from that which has not as yet happened.

LESSON THREE
Your brain, your body, and you

The mind and the body are very complex mechanisms. Great strides have been made in understanding them, but there is more that we do not know than we do know. The greatest problem rests with persons who are willing to work on premises that are out of date, and those who sincerely believe that they have found the "last word." We operate on the best knowledge available, and recognize that much of it will be proven false within our lifetime.

However, there are many things that seem relatively certain and have endured the test of time. The most notable is the holistic aspect of the mind/body and behavior. The mind is a concept set apart from brain. The concept of the soul is somewhere in there as well. The mind is not to be confused with brain; this will be explained later. The body must act in concert, much the same as a house. Think of a house as having many systems: that is, the electrical, the plumbing, the heating/air-conditioning, and many rooms. The body has the building, an electrical system, a plumbing system, a ventilation system, and many "rooms" - that is, sections to the body and brain. You might also consider your body much as does the automobile mechanic. An automobile has a circulatory system (radiator), ventilation system (fan-blade, heating/air-conditioning), a plumbing system (gas, oil, anti-freeze), and electrical system (battery and wiring), etc.

Just as in the automobile we cannot have gasoline in the radiator, and cannot have anti-freeze in the gasoline, the body cannot have blood where air belongs, and vice versa. This basic understanding is important to understanding the holistic nature of human functioning. You may say, "But what does this have to do with stage fright?" Stage fright, as has been stated, is not a singular item, but a combination of factors that come together at a "trigger point." The body is very similar. We don't want blood in the lungs and we don't want air in the bloodstream. Although the body has many parts that operate within their own system, none of them work correctly without the whole "machine" in harmony. A headache may be caused by dysfunction far away from the head, and likewise, a backache may be caused by an abnormality in the head.

When approaching stage fright, we must be willing to look at every aspect of human living. The causes are often hidden from plain view and only infrequently have a single cause. They are puzzles that must be put together – and put together correctly! When the pieces are put together wrongly, they do not fit; when forced into place, still do not fit, and do not make the puzzle's picture correct. Further, just like a puzzle, if you force something into place, damage is the result. This is the way the Creator designed the human body and its method of operation is holistically constructed.

There are three basic systems in the body: the electrical, the anatomical, and the chemical. These systems operate in tandem; they are inter-dependent. The electrical system operates the heart and the nervous system. The chemical system includes the hormones, the neurochemicals, and all of the basic balance of nutrients, vitamins, minerals, and oxygen/carbon dioxide. The anatomical system includes all the physical structures in the body that allow and inhibit physical movement and organ functioning.

These three systems are intimately aware of each other and are not easily fooled. They guard against outside invasion of everything from air pollution to bacteria and viruses. They allow us to be awake, to go to sleep, to be happy or to be depressed. They participate in activities such as how fast our heart beats to what we dream while asleep, and so much more that is unnecessary to discuss here. The important thing for us to know is that the body works as one mechanism at all times.

What changes how the systems work, alone or together? Disease, bacteria, viruses, fever, inflammation, edema, fractures, trauma, and other "direct" insults to the body are all capable of altering how we function. These are the more obvious causes. There are many less obvious causes that are, nonetheless, just as powerful - they are things like lack of sleep, improper diet, lack of exercise, insufficient hydration and stress. Then there are the factors that we might call "set-up" items: i.e., things that probably, by themselves, do not cause direct harm but produce a chain reaction that turns out to be damaging. And the damage is very hard to trace, since it came about by a chain of events. Some such items are estranged personal relationships, arguments, being too hurried, worrying too much, focusing on end results without looking properly at the means to get there, and many, many other less "tangible" events in our lives.

What does this mean for stage fright? It means that you can't "just be nervous." It means that when you are "just nervous," there is much more going on at the same time. Some of this is conscious and much of it is unconscious. That which is conscious is usually the least important part. Some of the time, when we know what is wrong, we can correct it. That which we do not know - in other words, that which is unconscious - we have to work to get at and do anything about. It often takes professional help.

The other aspect of "the person" that we must consider is the "soul." Some call it spirit, others the self or other rubrics; by any name, it is the part that houses our values, the presence or absence of our integrity, our spiritual orientation, and the "stuff that makes you, *you.*" Those who choose to deny or underemphasize this essential part of the human do themselves a grave injustice. This part is as essential to performance and the dealing with stage fright as the physical and psychological parts. The Wisdom literature (the Book of Proverbs in the Bible) tells us that what we think becomes us; in other words, you become what you think (Proverbs 23:7). The concept in that piece of wisdom is not anatomically based – it is not the brain. It is the mind. It is not the electricity in the body, the blood, or the way our physical parts are put together - it is derived from what we develop within our inner person as the true person.

What we read, what we watch, what we eat, our friends, the clubs we join, the churches we do or do not attend, the schools we attend, the medicines we take, and on and on, for multitudes of things, all contribute holistically to our "person."

Children become "wired" very early in life to sounds that are pleasant and those that are unpleasant. This is the simplest and probably the most accurate understanding as to why differing generations prefer very different kinds of music. That which is sonorous to one generation is cacophonous to the next. We also become accustomed to the sounds we hear, and eventually do not hear them. The great teacher of hypnosis, Milton Erickson, found while going to medical school and working nights that he got so used to the sound of the machinery that it actually put him to sleep. As a child, living only a few houses from the railroad tracks, I found that even a train whistle during the night did not awaken me.

There is a profound message in this concept. One of my dear trumpet friends grew up listening to the great operas and classical music, thus had developed a keen inner sense of musicality and proper interpretation - so much so that in his many years as a principal trumpet player for national symphony orchestras and playing under the baton of world famous conductors, none of them ever corrected his interpretation!

The opposite is, of course, also true. Children grow up hearing noxious sounds and accept them as "enjoyable" then continue to create sounds that only their genre seems to enjoy. It is true that differing styles of music express cultural and generational differences; however, each feeds the other - i.e., the artistic expressions help to create and sustain the culture, and the culture helps to create and sustain the expressions.

Again, though, what has this to do with stage fright? Look at the kind of sounds you incorporated into your memory in your developmental years. I find a huge difference in teaching those who have grown up with hard-rock, rap, and hip-hop type music than those who have experienced an earlier life of classical and pop. The feel for timing, expression, and musical dynamics, are all different. This is because the internal person, the unconscious mind, the real-self, has adopted a different concept for expression. Expression of what? The message. You will read in this text over and over again that all performance, whether speaking in public or playing Mozart on the piano, is an expression of a message, *your* message – your interpretation of someone's composition, probably many centuries ago. If speaking, you are re-interpreting the wisdom of the years in your own unique fashion. That's the message. No message – don't speak.

This lesson requires that we must see ourselves as a "whole" if we are to move on toward solving the problem of stage fright. In order to do so we must become very acquainted with our own body. There are persons who do not know they have a physical problem until the pain is quite severe because they are not "in touch" with themselves. It is important to "listen" to what your body is saying. For instance, the small, nagging ache in the back... Why is it there? Is it getting better or worse? Does it get worse when sitting or standing? And so on. Can you "get in touch" with your feelings so that you are aware of the difference between disappointment and depression? Do you really have a "stomachache," or is it a head problem – doing something or making a decision that you really don't want to do or make?

As you go through this book, you will need to heed each lesson seriously, since they all build on each other. To skip one or more, means potential failure. Why? Because we can only operate as human beings as a whole.

LESSON FOUR
The brain and its mechanics

Why does your brain and body fail you when you get on stage? This explanation is very simplistic. This "field guide" is exactly that, not a textbook. So, on we go to look at the brain and how it works in terms that everyone can understand. Since the very brightest minds don't know fully either, we won't be too upset if we are less than technologically and neurologically accurate all of the time. The aim here is to understand that, in order to conquer stage fright, we have to have a little understanding of why we get "nervous," and why the brain seems to go a different direction than we instructed it to go.

There are literally two brains – the left one and the right one. They are called hemispheres; the right one seems to be more involved with emotions, and the left one more involved with analytical thinking. This is entirely too black and white, since we know that each side can compensate and, when necessary, take over at least some of the functions of the other side. I have a trumpeter friend who, when his right hand was injured, learned to play the trumpet with his left hand quickly and expertly – his livelihood depended upon it. There are persons who, through trauma, have obliterated one side of their brain, and the other side took up many tasks from the other. The brain is a very adaptable organ indeed.

But for our purposes, let's stick with the simpler understanding. You could think of an artist as primarily "right brained" and a mathematician as "left brained;" but of course, that is only partially correct. Nonetheless, let's contrast it to a pipe-organ player who is managing two feet, two hands, ten fingers, two eyes, two ears, and a brain in concentration, all the time while turning pages, watching a conductor, coordinating with brass players, watching a choir, and trying to play with the emotionality intended by the composer! This is a poor, but maybe helpful, illustration of the incredibility of the coordination of left/right brain function.

The brain is the physical anatomical structure inside the cranium (skull), sitting in the head, balanced on the weakest and most flimsy part of the body, the neck. The neck and spine form the conduit through which runs the massive telephone and electrical wiring for the whole body. Injuries to that part of the body can render one paralyzed from the neck down. The mind is another matter altogether. It is the composite of abilities, feelings, emotions, and other imponderables that make us human rather than lower animals. The front of the brain - the pre-frontal cortex - in that part above and behind the eyes called the forehead, has in it the ability to act as executive administrator of the whole person. You could think of it as the CEO of your person. It manages all that is called human. That's the part that allows or prohibits us from expressing thoughts, feelings, sounds, or other human acts in inappropriate places. It acts as the adjudicator of social graces, appropriate behavior, scheduling, sorting out miniscule details, and allowing or repressing our urges.

We have spoken briefly about the two sides of the brain – that is, the two brains. A little deeper look will be helpful at this point. The left hemisphere (part) devotes much of itself to the way our body parts move - that is, the motor (moving) and sensory (feeling) parts. The amount of brain devoted to body parts is not at all proportional to the size of the body part. Many more nerves are devoted to the thumb and the tongue than to the pinky finger or little toe. And, for instance, the fingers have more nerve connections than the upper arm. You can see why there are five fingers on each hand, each with three distinct parts and three hinges called joints. They also have to be a major sensory input to be able to feel more acutely than the upper arm. It is also important to remember that we are "cross-wired," meaning that the left part of the brain controls the right side of the body and that the right side controls the left side of the body. For instance, a person who has a stroke of the right side of the brain may be paralyzed in the left arm.

Then there are the various parts of the "brain" that are actually outside of the head. This part runs down the neck and spine and has a web mechanism that goes to all the organs inside the body, the arms, and legs. The nervous system, as the whole structure is called, should be thought of as the central nervous system, and the peripheral nervous system. Now these are very complex, but can be made simple for our needs here. The central nervous system is largely the brain inside the head and the nerves that run up and down the spine. We have already seen how important the brain inside the head is; now we need to see the equally great importance of the peripheral system. That system is divided into two parts: the sympathetic and the parasympathetic systems. These are easy to understand for our purposes. The sympathetic system is the arousing part and the parasympathetic is the calming part. Now it's starting to make sense, isn't it? Stage fright doesn't stay in the head – it goes all the way to the finger tips and the organs inside our bodies. Now we know why we tremble, shake, sweat, or get light headed under stress and, guess what? Stage fright.

Stage fright, which is definitely a kind of stress, sends a message to the brain (actually the hypothalamus) which then sends telegraphs very rapidly to all the other organs to watch out for an invasion. This can be thought of as the sympathetic system, because, no surprise – it is sympathetic to our protection, hence it arouses (stresses) us. So, in the face of an enemy onslaught, the eyes dilate, blood pressure rises, muscles contract, blood vessels widen, the lungs work overtime, the heart beats faster and more vigorously, speeds us metabolism, sends messages to relax the bladder, and other physical reactions we don't need at that time. In other words, we prepare for war. Any wonder that in the face of a presentation or performance we are stressed? And imagine what the stress is like for us when there is inadequate preparation, poor environmental conditions, or if we have a cold!

The other part of the peripheral system is called the parasympathetic – i.e., "para" meaning "along side." It is the other half that can bring calming to the body. This in turn contracts the pupils, slows the heartbeat, stimulates digestion, contracts the bladder, and allows for free blood flow to all parts of the body. Remember that it's the blood that brings oxygen to the brain, and the nutrients for brain function, including memory.

Since many people literally shake when they have stage fright, we must take a brief look at the muscles of the body. Our musculo-skeletal system (muscles and bones) works very much like a block and tackle. You may have at one time seen an auto engine suspended on a couple of chains between pulleys. This is a block and tackle system. When one chain is pulled the other one has to relax, and when it relaxes, the other one must be stressed. Again, we see the human body. When we are tensed up on the stage, the wrong muscles are under stress and the ones that give you balance, equilibrium and an "at-ease" posture are tensed up. Wrong! Now of course, we don't want complete relaxation – you'd fall over. Some muscles must be tense, but they should not be the ones around the lungs, the neck, the shoulders, and other vital parts for our presentation. Brass players, for instance, need control of muscles around the mouth and throat (other parts too), and singers must have control, yet relaxation of the throat, vocal cords. And all who perform anything that requires breathing must have both relaxation and control of the lungs.

The lungs are worthy of a bit more discussion. When we over-breath - i.e., hyperventilate - we are upsetting the oxygen/carbon dioxide balance in the body. This has many ramifications, but short of ending up in the emergency room, it gives the performer the wrong blood-gas ratio for proper thinking, muscle control, balance, and, of course, breathing. Now we know why public speakers, musicians, and the like are always talking to us about proper breathing.

LESSON FIVE
Your chemical plant

We are massive chemistry laboratories. There are all kinds of chemicals, vitamins, and minerals - liquid, semi-liquid and solid - at work in us 24/7. The hormones that are produced by the endocrine glands are part of this system. They are particularly important for performers to understand, since their products are emptied directly into the blood supply - meaning that when stressed, those hormones are there "Johnny-quick." And, as importantly, most of them are controlled by the autonomic (automatic) part of the nervous system, therefore beyond our immediate control.

The autonomic (automatic) nervous system is kind of like the knee-jerk. When triggered, it goes into action, and once in action is almost impossible to control. The system is sometimes called the "fright, fight, flight" response. These are the sequential responses of the autonomic nervous system. You might think of them somewhat like the Three Stooges. Moe may be seen as the aggressor - that is, the cause of the fear. Larry got smacked all the time, but often struck out in the wrong direction - that is the fight. And Curly just tried to get away from it all, but rarely succeeded. Moe, Larry, and Curly = fright - fight - flight. They were ineffective totally. Moe's fear gave way to a series of comedies, Larry's defenses were ineffective, and Curly, in spite of it all, just couldn't get away.

The reaction caused by neurotic fear - i.e., "free floating" anxiety - is similar. The fear is really quite comical because it is irrational; the fight is ineffective because it is based on unrealistic information, and the flight doesn't work because there is no place to go. Irrational fear can only go to irrational places - i.e., the non-existent and imaginary.

Once we see anxiety for what it is, it ceases to have power. Irrationality, when exposed to reality, always gives way.

The absolute antidote for neurotic fear and anxiety is a fourth "F." Fright, Fight, Flight, and Faith! Faith is powerful and overcomes anxiety every time. Faith in one's self is paramount. Faith in one's teacher is essential. Faith in the audience is realistic. Faith in God is irreplaceable. Self-confidence is the root of performance confidence. One's relationship to his/her mentor or teacher is crucial. Recognizing that audiences do not want you to fail is clearly true. Faith in your purpose here on earth, your purpose on the stage, and recognizing that your talent was freely given to you by the Creator and that you now have the ability to send your message via voice or instrument is imperative!

The brain also makes every attempt to protect itself from physical invasion. Stress and excessive anxiety is interpreted in the nervous system as an attack. As a result, the neurological and chemical armies of the body get ready for war. Amazingly effective!

The brain produces its own narcotics. Yes, I did say narcotics. That is why a baseball player can literally sprain or even break an ankle and, without noticing the pain, run on into home plate. Then, of course, Yow! The endorphins, as they are called, mask noxious stimuli including pain. These natural body chemicals function under stress. Stage fright is stress; therefore, the endorphins are at work. This can be both good and bad. They can cause one to "get through" an otherwise physically challenging situation, but may also block needed sensitivity to bodily awareness.

When we look at the chemistry of the body – especially for that of the performer - we must talk about food, drugs, medicines, hydration, and air. First, food: there are foods that cause specific stresses for particular types of performance. There are too many to list, except to give an illustration. A singer is best not to drink milk or eat ice cream immediately prior to singing. Why? Milk products create thick mucous. Thick mucous coats the vocal cords, thus creating different frequency of vibrations - hence, a different sounding "voice." Brass players are also advised similarly, since mouthpiece playing relies upon natural mucous viscosity. Over hydration (too much water when playing) or under hydration (letting the body get too dry) does not allow for the natural mucous for the tongue and lips to work properly.

There are other foods – those that cause allergies – only known to the individual. Too much caffeine restricts the blood vessels and does not allow the free flow of oxygen; tobacco (which can't be good in any form) dilates the blood vessels and causes abnormalities in the "inner tube" (intima) part of blood vessels. Anything that disrupts the normal flow of blood and oxygen cannot be beneficial for anyone, particularly when under the stress of performance.

Medications are extremely important to discuss. Your physician and dentist must be told that you are a performer, of whatever sort. Modalities of treatment can be harmful to you without your health care provider knowing it. Wind instrument players need to be sure that their dentist knows the instrument they play.

Minor adjustments in the teeth and gums can result in massive changes in embouchure. Singers and public speakers (as well as most others) need to take a careful look at any kind of modality that inserts tubes or instruments into the throat, since injury to the vocal cords is easily done and not easily repaired. We need not say anything about illegal drugs, except, as you well know: Don't!

Some of the most troubling medications are the ones that people think are harmless because they are OTC; that is, over-the-counter. You can buy them without a prescription. Probably some of the most troubling are the antihistamines which cause drowsiness, dryness of body – particularly mucous – effecting the parts needed for speaking, musical performance, etc. Consult a physician prior to putting yourself on any medication; the ramifications are greater than you think, and can damage a profession.

A word about Beta-blockers is essential. Although there may be times when a seasoned professional may need to rely upon this kind of medicine, it should be the unusual exception and not the rule. Beta-blockers slow the heartbeat and make many changes in the electrical system of the body. A reason which is as important or maybe more so, is that young folks who find them helpful, will, by all likelihood, continue to increase the dosage to keep up with the increasingly body demand (as it gets accustomed to its effect and needs more for same level of action) until deleterious health problems ensue. And, although it sounds like an "old wives tale" (not all old wives tales are wrong), the kind of control it offers and the false sense of relaxation it brings often leads to the addition of other drugs, legal and illegal, including the addition of alcohol. This combination has been the end of many a musician's career.

The combination of medications, vitamins, and nutritional supplements all need to be discussed with your physician. Many things that we put into our bodies are basically "medicine," although not called that. For instance, eating too many carrots, believe it or not, can turn your skin yellow! Coffee, tea, and chocolate all have caffeine, which is also an ingredient in many medicines. Alcohol changes the way that almost everything is metabolized in the body. Many times alcohol will cause a medication not to work at all, and at other times causes the medication to become much too powerful. There are far too many illustrations of food and medication combinations that can cause harm to reference here, so it is of utmost importance to always ask the pharmacist about medications taken together and to be sure what they are for and how they work, when they are prescribed by your doctor. Some medications cause excessive dryness, others too much saliva. Some medications produce nervousness and cause irritability. Some medications make you drowsy and others make you jittery. Just remember that no medication, whether by physician prescription or over the counter, is without side-effects. That means that the medication causes the body to perform in ways other than the reason for which it is taken.

And remember that you know your body best, and must learn to be "body-aware" so that you can tell if a medication is bringing on other symptoms. When this occurs, your physician must be contacted as soon as possible. When major symptoms develop such as a very fast heartbeat, shallow or rapid breathing, rashes, vomiting, diarrhea, severe headache, or any other severe bodily function, no time should be wasted before going to the nearest emergency room.

LESSON SIX
Your electrical plant

Many people find it difficult to understand that the body operates on electricity, but it does. There is a tiny organ in the area of
the heart that is called the Bundle of His that actually sends out
electrical signals and helps to regulate how fast the heart beats.
The nervous system is like a system of electrical wires. You can
imagine seeing the electric poles along the highway and think
of impulses (messages) literally being transferred from one pole
to the next. These are called synapses, and the messages literally
jump from pole to pole by what is called salutatory action. Information you don't need, except to understand that once you send a
signal it cannot be recalled! For stage fright, that means that once
the signal is sent from the brain that you are nervous, it starts a
chain reaction that is unlikely to stop. And in the case of nerve
conduction, *cannot* be stopped. It's called the "All or None" law.
Now we know why it is so important to stop stage fright before
it happens.

Fortunately, signals can be monitored. There is a main station
that can modify the message sent – it is the brain! We can think,
we can reason, we can determine, we can prepare, we can control
much of what we think – therefore we can control much of what
we do.

Although sleep is not specifically part of the electrical plant, since
it is basically neurological in nature (and the nervous system is
certainly electrical), it is worthy of discussion here. Sleep is not
optional for good health. One hour of sleep before midnight has

been proven to be worth two hours of sleep after midnight - a tough situation for night-club and other musicians whose hours don't comply! Nonetheless, at all ages, and especially children through age 18, sufficient sleep is imperative for brain growth. The brain continues to mature until at least age 18, and sleep is the Repair Shop. Dreams are also important – not the conten, but the exercise of dreaming, which seems to re-set the neurological connections and re-arrange the learned material from the day. Sleep can be looked upon as the time when the night clerks come in and re-stack the shelves, sort the sales of the day, balance the books, and prepare for another business day.

LESSON SEVEN
The stages of performance anxiety

After observing student and professionals, I have established a useful scale to determine best how to help those suffering from this disorder. The stages are not absolute and often overlap each other. The suggestions for help at each stage also are not absolute, but are approximations, and the help suggested is not arbitrary. It is important, however, to see that the person helping in Stage One is not able to help in Stage Five, whereas the professional offering service at Stage Five may be able to offer help from Stages One through Five. There is no substitute for addressing the problem "head-on," then seeking the correct person to help you. Getting incorrect advice or treatment is often worse than getting none. Seek a second opinion when in doubt. Be honest as you look at these stages and see where you fit, if in any of them. If you are one of the fortunate persons who have never experienced uncomfortable nervousness when performing, be most thankful and commiserate with the rest of the performing world!

The following stages of performance anxiety should be considered as illustrations. None of them will fit you or your problem. But as you read them, you can see the kind of complexity that requires the greater and greater degrees of help that you cannot give yourself. Many readers will recognize that they were at one or more of the stages, and how they got through it. They will tell you the beautiful stories of how their teachers, their parents, their colleagues, and band directors helped them through crisis times. Others will not find that any of these stages fit them. There are many, many persons who never need the higher levels of outside help. However, many persons would have been and can now become far more excellent as speakers, singers, instrumental players, or performers, if they are willing to lay aside pride and concern for what others think and seek expert help. Professionals are confidential. Psychologists and psychiatrists, like all other doctors, take confidentiality seriously. They have been trained to know how to diagnose and treat your problem. Further, and very importantly, psychologists and psychiatrists are prepared to decide how much of a problem is "medical" and how much is "psychological" and refer you to the proper help. Many "problems" that look like they are "emotional" are rooted in physical causes, requiring a physician's knowledge. Others that look like physical problems are actually emotional and best treated by a psychotherapist. Licensed, Board Certified professionals can be trusted with the secrets that handicap you.

Don't think that you are "too good" not to suffer from any of these levels, but realize that you are indeed "good enough" to do so!

Stage One: Slight butterflies, some trembling; not disabling, only troublesome. Can become a friend by turning the anticipation into joyful excitement. Rarely, if ever requires help. Simple answers solve the problem.

Stage Two: Nervousness is more difficult to turn into joy; minor disturbance to performance. Simple answers don't work, or don't work consistently. Often requires assurance from mentor, teacher, etc. Simple advice, not serious counseling usually suffices.

Stage Three: Generalized nervousness; observable to self and others. Interferes with performance, but does not disable performer. Physical symptoms, emotional disequilibrium, and continued symptoms after performance. Requires coaching, usually from someone in the same field (i.e., musician performer, senior teacher, experienced guidance of some sort). More serious and cannot be ignored.

Stage Four: Specific nervousness, trembling, dry mouth or other disabling bodily functions; definitely interferes with performance, so much so that it is clearly noted by self and others; may actually interrupt or cancel performances. Exact diagnosis is necessary and specific help is recommended from Doctoral level psychologist or a trained experienced professional in anxiety disorders.

Stage Five: The most serious stage; immobility, cannot perform. Disabled prior to or upon attempting to perform. Requires professional help from Doctoral level psychologist, psychiatrist, or physician. May require psychological examination, medical examination, laboratory tests, to establish a specific diagnosis.

It is important further to be careful and obtain the level of care needed. Each stage utilizes a different kind of helper.

Stage One can benefit from a teacher or mentor who can make suggestions and model performance excellence.

Case Study: Joel is an eleven year old boy. He has worked hard to get ready for his speech on Lincoln for the special program of his Boy Scout troop. He has his notes prepared, he is dressed fit for the king, his hair is plastered down just the way his mother wants it, and even his shoes are shined. He isn't at all nervous. But just when he hears his name called, he starts to get the jitters, thinks he has to go to the toilet, and his face gets red. But, being the dutiful Scout that he is, he is "always prepared," as the Boy Scout oath requires. So he walks out on stage, almost trips over a chair-leg, drops his notes, and almost cries. But he recovers, picks up his notes and surprises himself by remembering the speech even without notes, delivers it actually quite well, gets a huge round of applause and leaves the stage visibly shaken, but having done well.

Stage Two can benefit from a coach or other person with experience in "stage fright" and performance problems.

Case Study: Kathy is a fourteen year old flute player. She has been playing for four years and this is her third public concert with the community orchestra. She has been playing the second part, but today the "first-chair" player is ill and she must play the first part. The orchestra leader has done well in suggesting that she also know that part, and she has practiced it well. She is nervous, shakes a bit, and her solo has a bit too much vibrato due to her nervousness. But, she doesn't blurt out any sour notes, and her orchestra mates, parents, and orchestra leader congratulate her and are proud of her. Kathy is disappointed in herself and starts to cry. She thinks she showed her nervousness, sounded "icky" on the solo, and "just knows" that her parents and others are telling her she did well just to make her "feel good."

Stage Three requires a more psychologically trained professional able to deal with stress, problem-solving, family, marital, school difficulties, and techniques such as the Alexander Technique, hypnosis, relaxation, and lifestyle counseling.

Case Study: Lisa is a bright and very attractive young lady, very gifted as a soprano singer. She has studied voice since she was nine and is now twenty-two. Her parents divorced when she was thirteen and she then went to live with her dad, who was financially supportive but overly critical of her academic and musical ambitions. He wanted her to become a nurse, or something that could "earn some money" since, as she could see, "marriages just don't work out." She had started to ruminate a lot, skip practice, and slouch as she walked. She began having difficulty sleeping and was "just not interested" in much.

Stage Four requires a licensed psychologist or psychiatrist capable of desensitization training, hypnosis, psychological testing, diagnostic interviewing, and rooting out the basic cause of the problem, as well as treating it.

Case Study: Mike wants to be a radio announcer, news-caster, or other media person. He was doing well until while in his internship at a local radio station: the control panel "shorted out," the radio went silent, the control panel was sparking with electricity, and the switchboard lit up with questioning callers. He panicked, fled the room, broke out in a cold sweat and urinated on himself. Now he cannot make himself return to the radio station even though his manager does not blame him, did not criticize him and did not in any way discipline him. As a matter of fact, the station is willing to help him in any way they can, because they believe he has "great potential."

Stage Five requires an experienced, licensed, psychologist or psychiatrist, capable of doing all of the items in Stage Four, plus the ability to do laboratory testing if necessary for physical causes of the problem, do in-depth psychotherapy, and prescribe medication if needed. This is the one place where the Beta Blockers and other anxiolytic medications can be useful.

Case Study: Bill is a seventeen year old percussionist. He is known in the community as one of the best on most any genre of music. He does well on tympani, snares, tom-toms, cymbals, and all of it. He even does well on the bars –i.e., the xylophone, marimba, and vibraharp. For the last five performances, ever since he and his girlfriend broke up and his father unexpectedly died, he has fallen apart, performed poorly, and seemed to be "in another world." He just can't concentrate, has lost interest in his music and seems to be becoming a "loner."

Understanding the levels of stage fright is essential. Honesty in self-appraisal and willingness to pay attention to what your body is "telling you" is imperative. Ask your teachers what they observe. Ask your peers what they observe. Have someone video your performance and watch it in the privacy of your own home. It is helpful to learn how to be self-critical without being self-depreciating. If you do not learn how to be honest with yourself, you will not improve. Others will be helpful, but often do not want to "hurt your feelings" or feel that their remarks might discourage you. When others give you their opinion, thank them; even if you think they are wrong, listen to them, and consider that they might be right. We can learn something from everybody, even those who are harsh and negative toward us.

LESSON EIGHT
Accepting the artist within you

Public performance of any kind is an art. The soul of the performer is bared in public. Values, beliefs, opinions, and spiritual underpinnings can be partially shielded, but by and large, we cannot keep ourselves (our true person) secret.

We have no trouble saying that a public speaker who has nothing to say should just shut up and sit down! The same goes for a motivational speaker, a singer, or an instrumentalist. Trumpet players are instructed to see the trumpet as a megaphone with valves. What you put in is only amplified, like a computer - "garbage in, garbage out." The primary task of an artist is to find the soul of his/her work, and find the medium for expressing it best to the audience. The public performer does this by attempting to look at the lessons to this point, apply them very personally, then find the balance of mind and body that will provide the best support for that expression.

The body can, and should be, a friend. It should not cough when you want to deep breath; it should not be too dry when you want to swallow; it should not be too wet so that you have only unnatural viscosity in your mouth to play a brass instrument; it should not tremble when you want composure; and so on. However, when we feed it the wrong stuff, insert the wrong chemicals, deprive it of sleep, and mistreat it, the body can become a formidable enemy.

The aim of any and all help in overcoming performance anxiety should be to help the performer literally "rise above one's self." This means that we must think of transcendence as the method for achieving the finest performance. In that state, one leaves the cares, the details, the environment, and even the techniques behind, and moves into a state of mind similar to meditation. When we watch the great musicians perform, it appears that they are nearly in a trance state and unaware of their surroundings.

Everyone has artistry of some sort in them. It is not always easy to find it, but we are God's creatures and each is made with special talents, gifts, and abilities. It is up to us to find those unique qualities, develop them, and use them for the benefit of others. It is said that Michelangelo was once asked what he was chiseling into the slab of marble. He is reported to have replied, "I am not chiseling anything into it; there is an angel in there that is trying to get out!" That's the way we are as marvelously built humans – there is a talent, a gift, or a unique ability that is in us waiting to be released. The humanness in us is announced with these wonderful unique qualities, unlike the animal world that do not have those abilities. We are able and are expected to discover these gifts and to use them in our own individual way. Often we hear a performer or speaker say, "You should have asked so or so to give this talk or play this performance." Such self-deprecation not only does an injustice to yourself but to those who requested your performance.

I was once asked to play trumpet for a performance. I did not know who would be in the audience, but I certainly did not expect some of my friends who were much more talented and experienced than I to be present! But, as we all learn, a promise is a promise, and regardless of what happens, "the show must go on." So I played - acceptably, I suppose, but certainly not as well as some of my teachers and more professional colleagues sitting in front of me. After the performance, as we are all prone to do, I apologized to them for a performance less than they would have done. One of the most experienced and well known of the group simply said, "Never apologize for what you have been asked to do. It was excellent, and further, they wanted to hear you. If they had wanted to hear one of us they would have asked us!" You are not usually requested to speak, play, or sing, because you are the finest in the world – you are asked because others want to hear what you have to say. And remember, we are "saying" whether singing, speaking, or playing an instrument.

The ability to rise above one's self is called transcendence. We transcend our own abilities when we are inspired with what we want to say. If the message comes deeply from within, the audience knows it. If we are simply playing notes or saying words or singing a song, there is no fire. More than once music adjudicators have given first place to someone who made a mistake but sent a message that was clear and sincere, as over against the one who may have played, sang, or spoken without making a mistake, but delivered a technical iceberg.

There is no one simple way to develop transcendence. It comes from a deep sense of purpose, self-confidence, inner-peace, knowledge of the material, experience, values, and having a soul-centered reason for doing what you are doing. When you cheer at a ball-game, you aren't nervous, you don't worry that others will think that you are too loud, or that your voice is too shrill. You are impassioned and yell it out. When you weep at a funeral, you don't worry that you may be seen. Grief is real, understood, and expected to be shown in the most human way. The same is true with performance. When you feel passionately about what you are doing and you are prepared to "cheer it on," the body and the mind cooperate with you. This is not to say that you cannot sabotage it. You certainly can, and many do. You can sit in the bleacher and feel passionately about who might win but refuse to let the emotion out. You can feel grief and stifle the tears. You can feel joy and inhibit the laughter. But all of this is abnormal and not the depth of humanness that is within you. Be a Michelangelo. Start chiseling to let your angel out!

LESSON NINE
How's your body?

Are you "body aware?" Meaning, are you in touch with your body? Do you recognize the early signs of fatigue, pain, or emotional distress? As a physician, I have seen many persons who did not recognize the messages their body was sending them until it was too late. Others, of course, recognize the early signs but ignore them. Either is self-destruction. Not all "early signs" develop into serious problems; as a matter of fact, fortunately most do not. However, over the long haul, when the same sign repeats itself over and over again, eventually, the "small sign" becomes one that gets your attention. For instance, the recurrent "heartburn" can eventually become a serious stomach ulcer, or even cancer. The repetitive hip pain can become a degenerative joint requiring an artificial joint.

Being aware of your body is absolutely essential for a career in any kind of performance. The early hoarseness for the singer, the recurrent lip pain for the brass player, or the nagging back-pain after standing for the public speaker, are all warning signs that the body needs attention. The body speaks, often softly at first, then more loudly, and eventually it shouts. Unfortunately, if we wait until it shouts, for some, the career is damaged beyond repair, and sometimes the body as well.

Let us first look as our general health. Do you usually feel energetic, lively, happy, in good physical condition, and ready to "take on the day?" If not, an appointment with a physician is in order. Laboratory tests may be necessary to determine such things as hypothyroid problems, blood-sugar levels, gastro-intestinal functioning, and much more. There are things you can look into the mirror and get some ideas about for yourself. For instance, how is your posture? Slouching makes for poor spinal alignment, hence poor circulation and poor neurological functioning. Shallow breathing - the "cigarette smokers puffing" - disallows adequate ventilation for the lungs, thus sequestering too much "bad air" and starving the brain and body of much needed oxygen. Dry skin from dehydration shows that the outside is putting on a slide show to show you what is happening inside – namely, too little water. When energy is lagging, sometimes it has to do with diet – too many "fast foods" and not enough protein and nutrients from vegetables and fruits. Swelling of the ankles is also an outside sign of not-so-good things that are going on the body, particularly the kidneys – early signs of many things, including high-blood pressure, cardio-vascular problems, and even congestive heart failure. It could just be too much salt in the diet. Elimination of water and waste from the body is important as well. These are only a few - a very few - of the many things your doctor will want to take into account when you are feeling draggy, "run down," or unable to perform at your best.

For excellence in performance and a release from the physical causes of stage fright, we must pay attention to vision and hearing as well as other bodily functions. Eyesight is crucial for the sight-reader of music, as well as for the speaker to read his/her notes. There are eye exercises that your optometrist or ophthalmologist can show you that will strengthen your eyes. There are actually some programs that are purported to lessen or even alleviate the need for glasses! Hearing is also crucial. Particularly to the musician who wishes to blend with other players, know whether the instrument is "in tune," and finely tune the tone and sound of the instrument. Care of the eyes and ears needs not be emphasized here. They are precious organs and should not be undervalued.

Exercise cannot be over-emphasized. However, like other things, even a great deal of exercise is not valuable unless done correctly, methodically, and with care. Strenuously over-exercising when "out of shape" often leads to physical and mental problems. Walking and swimming are probably the most beneficial exercises for those who use their bodies for speaking, singing, or playing an instrument. Lung development, deep breathing, posture, over-all muscle toning, and mental balancing all are enhanced by those simple exercises. Free weight lifting helps build specific muscles which may be important for various instruments – if I played a Sousaphone in a marching band, I'd want a lot of them! But for the most part, overall general physical muscle strengthening is desired.

Exercise also aids in straight posture building, assuming that one exercises correctly. Public speaking, singing, and instrument playing all require physical endurance. Only those who have endured a three or four hour "gig" can appreciate how tired the body can get when blowing, bowing, or playing drums. The seasoned minister or public speaker can appreciate the fatigue that comes in relatively short periods of time when being at one's best at a podium.

LESSON TEN
How's your brain?

The brain is a physical organ, like kidneys, liver, or heart. It requires blood supply, nerve stimulation, and proper exercise also. It can stagnate or be energetic. It can be quick or dull. We are not talking about IQ. The concept of IQ has long been outmoded except in the most constrictive or uninformed places. Anyone "smart enough" to sing, speak, or play an instrument has a brain that can be creative, expressive, and valuable. When you think carefully about the brain, just the ability to read, write, speak, and carry on a conversation requires an incredible amount of human ability. The brain has billions of cells and thousands of miles of neurological wiring – only a portion of which even the most accomplished geniuses of the world use. Further, it used to be thought that the brain stopped growing in childhood – this is no longer known to be true. The actual size of the human brain continues to grow until in the late teen or even early adult years. Further, it is not true that older persons cannot continue to learn and develop new skills. Believe it or not, "old dogs can learn new tricks."

However, this great functioning of the brain, its proper growth, and ability in old age does not occur all by itself. Careful, disciplined, habitual attention is necessary. We need to constantly ask ourselves if we are quick in observation. Are we keen in memory? Are we expanding our mind by "feeding" it good reading, healthy visual material, challenging ideas, and constructive criticism? As we get older, do we shut out new ideas? Do we refuse to understand new technology? Do we limit our mind-expanding activities? Or, as some in retirement villages are prone to do, literally rock themselves into the grave!

Do you want to keep your mind growing and stop the degeneration that comes with age? It can be done. Science is proving over and over again that the "mind at work" is the mind that slows the aging process. Constantly preparing new material, memorizing new music, learning new approaches for our performances, and keeping the bodily parts working in top shape for performance will all help to ward off brain degeneration. Further, we now know that the brain continues to repair itself, adapt to new situations, and even heals itself. This is called neuroplasticity. In simple terms, this means that the brain is doing its part in staying alive – we need to do our part to help it!

The brain as a physical organ requires a constant flow of oxygen rich blood, which means correct breathing; plenty of vitamins and minerals, which means eating vegetables and fruits; adequate protein, which means meat, cheese, nuts, and other protein rich foods; a goodly supply of hydration, which means drinking much more water than most of us do; and plenty of sleep and rest, which means 7-8 hours per night for most adults, more for teenagers, and even more still for children.

Great care needs to be taken of the head – the skull - that houses the brain. Concussions (hard hits to the head), contusions (slight tears in the lining of the brain), and other injuries can and do occur with great frequency. Contact sports, whip-lash auto injuries, and accidental blows to the head may result in loss of memory, confused thinking, headaches, blurred vision, dizziness, and many other symptoms, lasting from a few seconds to a lifetime. The brain is a precious organ – take care of it!

LESSON ELEVEN
How's your mind?

Although "mind" is a difficult thing to define, it is real. Sometimes it is spoken of as the "soul" of the person, or "the way we think." It is all that and much more. It is the manifestation of being a spiritual being. All persons are "spiritual"; they simply are not spiritual about the same things. To this writer, being spiritual is a belief that humans are made in the image of God and that we are created beyond human understanding. The mind represents the faith base that drives all of life. It is the starting point for the journey of life, which is a journey of faith. The Scriptures state that, "…faith is the substance of things hoped for, and the evidence of things unseen…" (Hebrews 11:1, RSV) This means that, although we may not be able to see everything with our physical eyes, we do "see" the substance - i.e., the real stuff - with our mind's eyes. It further means that although we can't always enter the evidence in a court of law, our mind "has witnessed it." Michelangelo's painting, The Creation of Man, demonstrates this beautiful concept with human and divine fingers reaching out to each other and nearly touching. Sometimes we "just know" that we are being propelled by "energy" greater than our own. The more spiritual a person thinks, the more apt he/she will be in recognizing this phenomenon.

One might ask, "What does what we believe, our values, our spiritual life, have anything to do with stage fright and performance anxiety?" The answer is incredibly simple and yet unbelievably complex. We cannot divorce what we think from the way we express ourselves. Hostile-thinking people come across differently than friendly persons. Persons who believe there is no "hereafter" live today differently than those who do. Performers who have something in their "soul" to say, say it differently than those who are searching for a message. Many of the great speeches were inspired by persons of great faith. Think of Abraham Lincoln, Billy Graham, or Martin Luther King. Much great music that is performed by believers and non-believers alike was, many times, composed for religious services. How many stop to think of what Handel was "saying" in his marvelous oratorio, The Messiah? Do the opera performers consider the words when they are singing Samson and Delilah? When the great organs shake the cathedral windows with the 32 foot bourdon pipe while playing a Bach fugue, does the audience realize that many of these great compositions were done by deeply spiritual persons and that the music was intended to glorify God?

One cannot be uncertain about basic beliefs and live effectively. The ship that is constantly shifting sails trying to find the wind often goes in circles. Everyone needs a chart, a compass, and one that is more accurate than directions given at the local convenience store. For this writer, such a compass is the Judeo-Christian way of faith.

Since the mind determines how we develop, what we consider important, what we hold as sacred, and what we believe will happen in the future, how can it not be of critical importance to anyone who stands in front of those who have come to hear a message? Being of faith does not mean that you never have doubts. Even Jesus' disciples had doubts, and one was reported as wanting to examine the nail-pierced hands before believing. We all join with the one who said, "...I do believe, help thou my unbelief." The issue is not whether we always have absolute certainty about the unknown. The issue is whether we recognize that we are not in control, and that a spiritual power much greater than us is in charge. When the latter is true, we can step to the stage with a positive message, a physical presence, a confidence based in much more than ourselves, and literally let go of the apprehension and anxiety.

The great Apostle Paul, (who, by the way, preached to thousands) on Mars Hill, said, "…laying aside every weight that so easily besets (sidetracks - *my word*) and with patience run the race that is set before us…). The wisdom of these words for the performer is deep, profound, and extremely helpful when taken to heart. This literally means that we drop the worries, fears, and focus on the goal, not letting disturbing things come in the road of reaching the excellence in performance we know our Creator and our audience deserves. It further means that we are very human and must take patience very seriously. Baby steps are not bad steps. Who ever heard a parent say, "Wow, that was such a small step that our baby took and then he had to fall?" No way, the proud parent gleams with every small step and watches in anticipation of the longer, more stable steps.

This is what great teachers do for their students. They are rewarded by the growth of a student. They do not look at the mistakes as negative fodder; but rather, they find the faltering baby step as a platform for the next, the next, and the next. That is why every performance is important. That is what makes every note a solo. That is why parents gloat over their child's home run, soccer goal, or good report card.

We are brain-washed into thinking that "it is not whether we win or lose, but how we play the game." This is totally untrue. If we do not play to win, we will lose, thereby once again proving the truth of unfilled prophecy. In other words, if we do not play to win, we play to lose, then when we lose, and we have won our own game of self-defeat!

Simply because we "play to win" does not mean that we can bully others, cheat, cut corners, and become arrogant. It means that we do our best and encourage everyone else to do the same thing. If we do not do our best and the other team wins, they do not win because of doing their best, they win by default, only because we "gave away" the game. When this happens, nobody wins and nobody feels good about it.

The mind must be balanced. One should not think more highly than he ought, the Scriptures remind us; however, by the same token, we are not called upon to be "door mats" for others to trample upon. We are confident in ourselves because we serve a higher calling and become "instruments" in the Creator's hands. St. Francis of Assisi prayed that we might be "instruments of peace." That concept is so helpful to the public performer. It takes the focus off of us and our human failings, and allows the performance to become the message that we are giving for someone else! We are the messenger, the announcer, the one that comes out on stage to introduce the real performer. This is important because when we feel the billion-watt spot light is centered only on us, we tend to either get the "big head" or we "crawl into the corner." Either reaction is neurotic, self-centered, and bound to failure. The person who diminishes him/herself into less than he/she is, believe it or not, is taking a liberty with their God-given talents and person - which is just as self-serving as the one who becomes over-confident and arrogant! Either approach is unfair to yourself, your teachers, your audience, and, most of all, your Maker.

The mind becomes the message. That is, we become what we think. If we think we can't do something, we are usually correct – and the mind and body see to it that we are right. There is the "I can," the, "Maybe," and the, "I Can't" kind of mind. The "I Can" mind is willing to accept small successes and appreciates the joy of the journey to the major accomplishments. The "Maybe" mind is always apprehensive. Success comes as a surprise – accepted, but not expected to be repeated. Everything is tentative. The "I Can't" mind does not plan for success, but instead, all of the energy is used up proving that it is correct in not succeeding.

We all need to call upon "outside resources" for excellence in anything we do. We all stand on the shoulders of those who have taught us and who have modeled our skill for us. The spiritual person is able to call upon an inner strength that comes from firm inner convictions and beliefs. Illustrative of this is the statement by St. Paul that, "I can do all things through Christ who strengtheneth me," (Philippians 4:13). This statement needs to be correctly understood. Paul was not gloating, nor was he boasting, nor was he showing arrogance or superiority. He was stating a truth that each of us need to put in our performance strategy: "I can do anything that I am called upon to do if I do not rely only on my humanness and get buried in my own limitations and past failings. Therefore, I have a strength that is greater than my own that will enlarge my abilities and deliver the message far better than I can do it in my own strength." It may well be that persons of spiritual heritage other than mine can do the same – I am only acquainted with my own Christian moorings and experience, thus the Apostle Paul makes sense to me.

People become "fixed" in the way they think. You can plan on their way of thinking, because it is "always the same." A patient once said to me that his son was absolutely unpredictable in that he could not count on him for doing the right thing. He was wrong. His son was totally predictable to do the wrong thing! Our brains establish patterns such as optimism, pessimism, being argumentative, being overly-complacent, becoming worrisome, or sometimes, boisterous, disruptive, attention-seeking, or egotistical.

The well-functioning brain seeks continuous learning. It seeks alternatives when frustrated or inhibited. It is capable of being self-critical without being self-deprecating. It sees the difference between fear and hope – these are the two opposites of failure and success. Fear is disabling and obliterates hope. Hope shines through the darkest night and allows one to see the damaging effects of fear. The Psalmist tells us, "In what time I am afraid, I will trust...," speaking of trusting God. Good advice.

There are many techniques that are helpful to building a healthy mind. Among the most productive are meditation and prayer. This is not the place to give a discourse on either of these, except to say that they allow one to enter the inner sanctum of the self in relation to the Creator and others, thus bringing equilibrium to mind, soul and body. Professional psychologists and psychotherapists utilize "guided imagery," which is also useful. Hypnosis, when used by expertly trained professionals, is also at times useful. A word of caution is in order, however. Learning to "hypnotize" someone is an easy task; knowing how, when, and why to use it is something else entirely. It can be compared to one who gives "a shot" - an injection of medication. Most anyone can learn quickly how to operate a syringe and needle. But knowing what to put in it, where to inject it, the side effects, possible toxicities, and how much to use takes professional training. Safety suggests that for any psychotherapeutic treatment, a licensed, Board Certified, person be enlisted. Too much care cannot be given to being in the "right hands" when dealing with the mind.

Values, beliefs, spiritual depth, and discipline in living an honorable life are the foundation blocks of a productive, healthy, well-balanced mind. Many performers think that what they believe does not affect their message. Wrong - so very wrong. Audiences are perceptive, and usually understand the "meta-message" better than the performer. The "meta-message" is that underlying story, hidden to the performer, that gets told whether intended or not. Inflection of the voice, raising the eyebrows, smiling, frowning, a shrug of the shoulders, or many other body-language manifestations "give you away," regardless of how much you attempt to masquerade! So it is better to have the healthy lifestyle, the honest mind, and the strong value-based beliefs, than to have to pretend, only to be shown up after all.

LESSON TWELVE
How's your performance?

All performances are big – none are small, none are insignificant. Whether it is a five year old playing a first piano recital, singing in a children's choir, or reciting a poem – it is a big occasion. We grow up building one big performance upon another. They are all big to the performer – or should be. Every performance is like every note in every song – each one is a solo. Once it is sung, played or spoken, it cannot be retrieved – it is final. That's what makes every performance important. We learn from our mistakes – both the successes and the mistakes can become positive in the mind. Even the worst mistake becomes a positive building block when viewed correctly. In fact, we learn far more from our mistakes than from our successes. There are several very sophisticated psychological reasons for this that are far too extensive and complicate to go into here, plus, they are not important – except to know that it is how we look at the mistake that counts. Performance success and the control of stage fright build on both successes and failures placed in the mind like Lego parts - one on top of the other, but in proper position.

We must learn to be honest in our self-appraisal. We must be able to look ourselves in the eye in the mirror and adjust our thinking without demeaning ourselves. We can ask honest questions such as: "did I practice enough – honestly?" "Am I technically able to do what I am attempting?" "Did I choose a piece of music, a speech, or a song, that is beyond my current level of competence?" And we must honestly admit whether we are performing for ego-building or for the right reasons.

The professional performer is ethical. There are rules, proper etiquette, respect for others, team-work, collegiality, and commonly understood practices that must be given attention. Showing up barely in time to perform is poor form, as is not being ready for the unexpected (which always occurs): the wind blowing your notes or music away, the stand collapsing mid-performance, a kid screaming bloody murder while you are speaking, etc. I was recently giving a master class/performance workshop at a high school when, in the middle of it, just as I really wanted the audience's attention, the fire alarm went off – twice! General adaptability without becoming flustered is essential. The audience depends on you to bring them back to normalcy; you are the one in front – the de facto leader.

This is where we strive to become the best that we can be at whatever level we are at that time. We put ourselves in situations where we are held accountable. We place ourselves beside those more experienced than we are. We seek and honestly accept positive constructive criticism. We thank those who mentor us and prod us on to our very best!

LESSON THIRTEEN
On seeking help

As has been stated, we cannot be too careful when we seek help. All helpers are not equal; in truth, some, although rarely intentionally, are more hurtful than helpful. Seeking help for physical and/or psychological challenges requires diligence and careful investigation. There are actually persons educated beyond their intelligence! The important thing for a professional to know is what he/she does *not* know. Someone has said that "true ignorance is not what we do not know, but what we know that is not so." Think about it. When we think that what we are doing is right, it becomes "right." Do not be afraid to get a second opinion. Do not be afraid to ask if the professional is a specialist in your problem. Do not hesitate to ask if your doctor has seen this problem before. Never be embarrassed to ask for credentials. A psychologist should have either a PhD, or a PsyD degree, licensed by the state, and preferably have ABPP (Board Certification) behind his/her name. Physicians will have either an MD or a DO degree, and again, board certification for their specialty. Those administering anesthesia will either have a DO, MD, or CRNA behind their name, and again, with appropriate board certification. When seeking help with vocal cords, a specialist who also sings or understands your needs if you are a public speaker may be your best bet. When having dental work, the wind instrument player definitely needs to be sure that the practitioner understand how a very tiny change in the teeth structure can change your embouchure. The anesthetist/ anesthesiologist needs to know that you depend on your vocal cords to pay their bill!

There are many more illustrations, but I am sure you get the picture. Whenever possible, seek the combination of professional skills you need, rather than having several specialists, each tackling a piece of the pie and none of them knowing the whole picture.

Be sure to study carefully the stages of performance anxiety previously discussed in this book and with your teacher, mentor, or another professional person. Honestly see where you fit, then seek the level of professional assistance appropriate to that level. Once you have found the professional whose expertise you need - and one with whom you can have the "right chemistry" - do not stop before the treatment is completed and you have accomplished your goals. Doing so can actually set you back and make matters worse.

Remember that a proper diagnosis leads to a proper treatment. The diagnostic phase is sometimes slow and tedious, but it is crucial. Work with your professional with all the insight you have and do not be afraid to share your observations, what you see as happening, or not happening, and any suggestions you might have. Competent professionals are not intimidated by honest help from their patients/clients. You have a right to ask for credentials, past experience, fees, expected outcomes, confidentiality, and availability. Do not settle for less.

LESSON FOURTEEN
The last lesson this semester

This may be the most important lesson so far. It is your decision whether you wish to undertake the disciplined approach to life that will equip you to do what you wish to accomplish. If you decide to depend on luck – well, "good luck." If you decide to depend on others to teach you, you will be disappointed. Others can show you how to teach yourself – they can model for you, they can encourage you, they can constructively critique you – but in the end, you must take what others give to you and literally teach yourself.

Performance, as you may have gathered from reading the previous lessons, is not a single item. It is the compilation of all that goes into a healthy lifestyle, a positive attitude, practicing beyond what others practice, and literally becoming all you can become in every phase of life. Performers often make it to "the top" only to topple off the pinnacle because the rest of their life is in shambles. One cannot survive on talent alone. And as we know so well, sports figures, musicians, movie stars, and public figures "hit the skids" - not because they are not talented, successful and even wealthy – but because the rest of their life does not support excellence in life, but instead supports failure!

This booklet is intended to offer *help* to find the answers – not the answers. Your answer is highly individual and uniquely yours. The answer for someone else may not only be the wrong fit for you, but it may make things worse. For instance, we know that trumpet players, for instance, seek the "silver bullet" in a new mouthpiece or some other "thingamajig," when it is the discipline of practice that is needed. Everyone in performance seeks the simple way – but there are no simple ways. If there were, everyone would be a star.

Hopefully, you will strive to become a whole person: that is, one whose life tells the wholesome story that you want to give your audience in performance. Your sincerity, your honesty, and your "realness" or "fakeness" will be perceived early on by your audiences. Becoming a performer, regardless of what kind - whether in singing, sports, or public speaking - is a solo journey. Others will join you to make the road more pleasant, but in the end, it is your trip, and how you prepare for it and walk it day by day is up to you.

THE FINAL EXAM

Look at each item and honestly evaluate your self against these suggested principles:

It is good to practice in front of a mirror, and it is good to talk to yourself in front of a mirror about the items in this "final exam." It is better that we judge ourselves before an audience does! My suggestion is to take one item per day. Don't attempt to go through the whole list all at once. To do so will encourage less than an in-depth look and tends to allow for less than full personal honesty.

Think of each item as a daily personal devotional introspection, meaning that you "reverently" evaluate yourself. Think about it at various times in the day. Then take stock of the aspects that you feel you do well and congratulate yourself for them – maybe have a piece of chocolate! Then take stock of those aspects that need more work. When these are discovered make a list – a real list. Write it down. (It always helps to put something down on paper and read it over several times.) Then ask yourself how you can start fixing it. If you can't come up with a satisfactory answer (and you'll know whether it is a good answer or a cop-out), seek help.

You can seek help in a similar way as looking at "The Stages of Performance Anxiety" in this book. Small concerns may be addressed by your teacher, mentor, or sometimes even a friend. But as you move up the ladder of difficulty, more advanced assistance is needed. If it is professional help, do not hesitate. Seeking help does not demonstrate weakness but strength.

1. Practice, Practice, Practice. Until you can recite, play or sing your presentation perfectly in your own studio or office, it is not ready for public performance.

QUESTION: Is my practice concentrated, intentional, regular, and consistent, or is it less than "smart practice" – sometimes, in truth, just "goofing off?"

2. Look into your soul and see if you really have something to say. That is, does the speech, the piece of music, or the poem, present a message from your heart? In music, do you know who composed the piece, why, when, and what for?

QUESTION: What is the central message I want my hearers to get from my performance?

3. Stand against a wall with shoulders straight back and pay attention to your posture. Do your shoulders droop and your midsection pouch out?

QUESTION: What does the way I walk, stand, or a gesture tell the audience?

4. Take a deep breath. Does it inflate your rib cage, or is it just from the shoulders up – the proverbial cigarette smoker's "puff-puff?"

QUESTION: Is my breathing controlled, or does it look like I'm about ready to collapse and need someone from the audience to come to my aid?

5. Close your eyes. Look at a center point in the middle of your

forehead. Keep centered there and see if you can feel serenity and composure. Thank God for the talent you have been given and the opportunity to share it with others.

QUESTION: *Have I honestly thanked God for my talent and the opportunity to deliver a message greater than my own?*

6. Sitting in a straight chair, count slowly to ten. With each count, breath slowly in and slowly out. And, with each breath start to relax from the top of your head to your toes.

QUESTION: *Have I taken time to pray, meditate, and look both inside and outside of myself on a regular basis?*

7. Refrain from excessive sugars, caffeine, and unnecessary medications prior to practice and performance. Alcohol and tobacco are serious deterrents to excellence in performing.

QUESTION: *What are the handicaps that I have put in the road that hurt my performance?*

8. Put your performance into a structured practice routine. Brass players should practice for 10-15 minutes then rest for the same amount of time. Treat the vocal cords and embouchure as you would training any other body muscle – repetitions not weight. And never overdo, since you can undo what has been done.

QUESTION: *Am I practicing "smart" and taking time between practice-parts to relax, think, and see the greater picture of what I am doing?*

9. Practice smartly. Much practice produces little if done incor-

rectly; actually, sometimes less than nothing. Practicing a mistake will guarantee a perfect performance of that mistake. I have heard many mistakes played perfectly!

QUESTION: *When I make a mistake and cannot get it "right," do I skip over it, seek help to correct it, or does my pride get in the road of growth?*

10. Enjoy what you do. When performance becomes work it is time to quit. The audience will know whether you "are in it" or just "putting it on."

QUESTION: *Do you honestly enjoy what you are doing and can you portray that joy to others?*

SUGGESTED READING

Ayers, A. Jean, Sensory Integration and the Child. Los Angeles: Western Psychological Services, 1979

Blacking, J., How Musical is Man?, University of Washington Press, Seattle, 1973

Campbell, Don G., Introduction to the Musical Brain, 2nd Edit.. MMB Music, St. Louis, 1992

Cox, Richard H., Issues of Life, InSync Press, Sanford, FL, 2001

Cox, Richard H., Managing Your Head and Body so You Can Become a Good Musician, 3d. edit., Colorado School of Professional Psychology Press, Colorado Springs, CO., 2006

Doidge, Norman, The Brain That Changes Itself, Penguin, New York, 2007

Goode, Michael I., Stage Fright In Music and Its Relationship to the Unconscious, 2nd edit., Trumpetworks Press, Oak Park, IL 60301, 2003

Hickman, David, Trumpet Pedagogy, Hickman Music Edition, Chandler, AZ, 2006

Knoblauch, Steven H., The Musical Edge of Therapeutic Dialogue, The Analytic Press, Hillsdale, NJ, 2000

Levitin, Daniel J., This is Your Brain on Music, Plume, New York, 2006

Lewis-Lucinda, Broken Embouchures, Oscar's House Publishing, NJ., 2002

Schneiderman, Barbara, Confident Music Performance, MMB, St. Louis, 1991

The Holy Bible Particularly the Proverbs, Psalms, Sermon on the Mount, and Paul's writings to the Philippians.

ABOUT THE AUTHOR

Dr. Richard H. Cox writes from a broad range of experience covering more than fifty years in several professional fields, including medicine, psychology, theology, and music, and is widely published in each of these disciplines. As a performer in each of these fields, he has gained a wealth of information to assist others facing the challenges of public performance. Dr. Cox is a regular presenter/performer/speaker at national and international venues including Interlochen Center for the Arts, the National Trumpet Competition, colleges and universities, and many religious organizations. He holds earned doctorates in medicine, psychology, and theology, as well as three honorary doctorates and numerous certifications and diplomate designations.

His breadth of clinical work with performers has included those with physical challenges including bodily deformities, post-traumatic disorders, post-surgical rehabilitation, emotional challenges, and a very broad spectrum of persons facing stage fright problems, who wish to evidence excellence in performing. Among persons seeking assistance have been musicians, public speakers, ministers, athletes, singers, musical directors, and actors.

He continues to welcome those who wish to pursue their performance and overcome stage fright and other challenges that prevent their ambitions from being realized.

www.ingramcontent.com/pod-product-compliance
Lightning Source LLC
LaVergne TN
LVHW021622080426
835510LV00019B/2718